LIKE IT OR NOT

Contents

Introduction ix

The Poems
   Identity and Individuality..*1*
   Relationships and Love...*27*
   Creativity *75*

User Guides 99
   Youth Guide *99*
   Parents Guide..*104*

Appendix A—Short Prose and Beginnings 109

Appendix B—Writing in Anger 115

About the Author 119

Index of Poems by Year 121

Introduction

As a child, I was small for my age, but I was placed in classes with kids who were one and sometimes two years older than I was. Sadly, I was not a gifted athlete like my sister, and I also refused to lower myself to be part of the "in" crowd. Sometimes I even thought that I must be crazy because I fought so hard to be different than what was the norm.

I did however have three things going for me: a wide-ranging vocabulary, a vivid imagination, and the desire to express myself. I had been reading difficult passages since before I had even begun to attend school, and was eventually tested as having a high school reading level when I was only in grade two.

I entered my first poetry contest at the County Library before I was even in my teens.

Words, poems, and eventually songs became my output, not only in place of scoring goals, baskets, touchdowns or homeruns, but also as my own personal path through my lonely and often confusing teenaged years. High school and early adulthood were difficult times full of challenging new emotions, and I usually picked up my pen to make it through those rough times.

Years later, having spoken with teens, parents, colleagues, and even some of those people who I thought "had it all together" in high school, I realized something: we all faced the exact same things as adolescents.

Some of these people had tried to face those challenging times with alcohol and drugs, others by outright rebelliousness, and even the top athletes and the "coolest of the cool" had to face their fears once the cheers and adulation were gone. Sometimes those same people faced those fears in the most difficult ways possible.

These days, youth face huge challenges while growing up: violence, drugs, alcohol, suicide, bullying, the pressure to do well at school, and the even stronger pressure to conform to a group identity. A personal outlet is needed.

This book therefore has two main purposes:

1) To let you know that although the feelings and fears that you as an adolescent or young adult feel are unique to you, you should know that the experiences that cause those feelings are universal. Your friends experience them (whether they admit it or not), your parents went through

them (although you might not believe it), and someday your kids and grandkids will too; and,

2) To show that poetry and prose are useful, valid, healthy, personal ways to express your entire range of emotions: fear. Anger, confusion, love, hate, longing, and even a simple desire to be creative;

These poems are grouped by subject matter, and are therefore not in order of when I wrote them. They do however range from about age nine to about age twenty. Sometimes poems can fit into many categories, but they have been placed in that which seems to best fit.

The first section relates to "Identity and Individuality", as throughout this time period, teens are troubled by trying to find a sense of themselves as people different from the family unit.

The second (and by far the largest) section includes poetry and prose about "Relationships and Love". Through our teen years, our relationships with our parents, classmates and other people are changing drastically. "Like", "love" and "lust" are often the most confusing elements of our entire life, but it is even more pronounced in our teenage years.

At times, we are trying to be one hundred per cent creative in our expressions, and the third section simply called "Creativity" includes those poems that do not fit into the other two categories. To be truthful, many of the poems in the first two sections are purely fictional and creative, but they do at least fit into a subject. The poems in this section however do not have a direct correlation with the other subjects.

Much of the poetry included is considered to be somewhat related to "classical" styles of poetry, using certain rhyming patterns and flow. These are the styles of poetry we tend to be taught in high school English classes, and because of that, they are easy to learn and use. Some are based on song formats instead, which makes them even easier! Music has always had an important role in my life, and it is very soothing to suddenly hear a song that exactly matches your mood and concerns. It can be even better when you can write a song yourself.

Scattered throughout the sections you will find some poems that were written in French first, with an approximate English translation. French is a second language to me, learned while at school. I believe that any time you can be creative in a second language, you are well on the way to fluency in that language.

In the appendices, you will find two separate sections: The first, "Short Prose and Beginnings" includes a variety of short story-based free verse, and some incomplete poems and writings. Appendix B has been kept very separate on purpose. This series of prose were written in about a half-hour during a period of anger, and get the very simple title of "Writing in Anger". They have been kept separate to show that anger is a very valid emotion, and that using writing to diffuse and express that anger can be very helpful.

In the long run, I am sharing my personal writing with you. These poems are taken directly from the literally hundreds of pieces of lined notepaper, memo pads, perforated computer paper, and even small scraps of pre-used paper that were at-hand when the poem first came into my mind. They are unchanged from the original feelings and intent that led to the poem in the first place, so they are truly the unpolished writings of a teen.

Just like talking to someone about a problem, sharing your personal thoughts can have a "healing" effect for all of us. To share or not to share your poems is always your personal choice, and I have chosen to finally share mine with you.

Hopefully they will truly inspire you to find *your* creative outlet.

So, put down the video game, and drop that can of spray paint. There are better ways to express yourself. Anybody with a pen and a scrap of paper can start to turn emotions into something constructive.

What you write is yours, and it is nobody's business but your own.

(Parents, you might want to turn to the "Parents Guide" section now. If you are giving this to your son or daughter, this may be the last time you see this book, and that is not a bad thing!)

IDENTITY AND INDIVIDUALITY

The search for a personal identity is often a lifelong, continuous pull between being "like them" and being "unlike them." For example, we spend a good number of our childhood years trying to be *like* our parents, but then seemingly twice as many years trying to be completely *unlike* them. We often lose our sense of individuality by trying to grasp a group identity, creating inner confusion as we try to separate self from others. No matter what, just be yourself!

Reality
©1984

Ah. Yes!
We all have eyes,
But can we really see?
We all have lips,
But can we really tell?
We all have ears,
But can we really hear?
We all have a heart,
But can we really feel?
We all have touch,
But can we really sense?
We all have a brain,
But can we really know?
We all have wants,
But can we really need?
We all have a life,
But can we really be?
Ah.

The Quest
©1977

I love my mother.
She always wants what is best for me:
"Eat your broccoli,
Be home at nine."
But I have a Quest.

I love my father.
He too wants the best for me:
"Do well at school,
Get a good job."
My Quest lurks in the dark.

So I try my best,
But sometimes the Quest gets in the way:
I do my work
The way I know how.
The Quest silently creeps up on me.

I try to excel.
I do what I can to move up:
I get involved,
Things go well.
The Quest starts to get in the way.

The day has come!
The Quest jumps out at me
And possesses my soul.
My body tingles.
The Quest is alive!

The Quest uses me.
It occupies my every moment.
It builds up inside me,
Throbbing, growing, living.
The Quest is me! I am the Quest!

John R. Palmer

The tension mounts.
My nerves are shot.
The Quest grows hungrier and hungrier.
I quietly hold out.
The Quest is on the run!

I am confused,
And quite dumbfounded.
In a fight to the death
Between me and the Quest,
The Quest is defeated.

Pain floods through me.
I feel so lost.
I have a great emptiness inside me.
I am not complete.
The Quest is dead;
      I am dead.

John's note: I have to admit, I was only nine when I wrote this poem, so I was not quite a teen (this might explain the comment about broccoli). By age nine, I was already questioning my individuality–having been placed in classes with kids two years older than me, my early "crushes" on girls, and possibly misplaced feelings were already a confusing part of my life, and I was emotionally unprepared. I can admit now that I was also a major annoyance to some classmates. Rejection and being shunned were already part of my life, and I was already beginning to write about it.

The Eagle Inside
©1985

The Eagle is born.

You care for me,
You comfort me,
You call me an equal.
As life goes on,
Both you and I
Can feel the same.
The eagle learns to fly.

You control me.
You whistle, I come.
You train me.
The more freedom I gain,
The more you tie me
Down to your perch.

Without warning,
The Eagle will rise again!

Real People
©1985

Fools!

Yes, you are all so blind
So as not to see the real me.

You who see me as a fool
Are but fools yourselves.

En garde!

Stop!
Think now John, think.

If they can't see the real you,
How do you know
That you can see
The real them?

Like it Or Not

I Don't Need You
©1987

I am resplendent in divergence!
I refuse to be like you and all your kind.

I am me, you aren't.

These times I spend alone
I spend withdrawing into my mind.

Far from you, very far!

Here I can spend time
How I like to, how I want to.

Alone; in my world.

There's only room for one
In my head with me—she's not like you.

She cares; you don't.

None of you can see me
For what I can do, only what I can't.

She does. She knows.

You all know who you are
Who spite me just for the sake of spiting me.

I hate you, all of you.

You love it, you lust for it:
The smell of my blood drives you to frenzy.

Slice my throat and feed.

John R. Palmer

Try as you may, you can't kill me
For life flows through me though I am drained.

Because of love, I live.

Sommes-nous individuels?
©1986

La vie.
C'est chère sur son âme.
On ensuit les faux
Et les vrais sont misent en boites.

On deviens méchaniques
Pendent que les vrais deviennent individuels.
Sont-ils fous?
Ou sommes nous?

Are We Individuals?
Translation ©2006

Life.
It's hard on your soul.
We follow the fakes
While the real people are locked in boxes.

We become robots
While the real people become individuals.
Are they crazy?
Or are we?

I Stand
©1987

I stand alone
Lonely and alone
This is not my home.

I stand before thee
Arms open to thee
Where should I be?

I stand strong
Inwardly strong
Where do I belong?

I stand in the snow
I love the snow
Now where should I go?

I stand with you
My friend, you
What should I do?

I stand broken
My nerves, broken
No further ahead than before I'd spoken.

Mirrored Life
©1988

Don't ask me
What I'm doing to my life
Because I don't know!

What can be misconstrued
Will be misunderstood.
Nothing can change that.

Two sides of a life
Not quite opposite,
Or even attracted by opposites.

But still a lifelong battle
Between different factors,
Each controlling a different path.

Side one is greed,
Of lust and of foolishness;
Not bad, just childish.

Escaping from a life
Of protectionism and perfectionism
To do wild and crazy antics.

To follow a path
Not dark, just dim;
An honest rebelliousness.

Side two is of power
Through social conscience
And social consciousness.

Knowing what's right
And practising perfection,
Gaining power and respect.

John R. Palmer

Knowing how to manipulate
Letting the people hear and see
What they want t hear and see.

But yet a side
Of responsibility and love;
True love and respect.

Where what's right and honourable
Is the road that
Life must follow.

To do all that one can
For one's fellow man
And the one he loves.

Giving all of himself
Until he kills himself
Through sheer martyrdom.

But do those
Whose lives he loves
Realize his sacrifice?

    These are not sides one can change
    Their actions cannot be stopped
    Each one acts of its own
    Give and take, take and give.

    Though flawed and shallow
    Each may seem to have no future
    But, could they come together?
    Childishness and responsibility

    One could live a perfect life,
    But yet purposely flawed
    To make it one we could all live.

The Blind Man
©1988

Listen:
Life isn't easy sometimes,
We all know that.
And I'm not one to talk
Like some demi-god
Besmirching his mortals below.

But like the blind man
Who'd seen his fill of the world
And no longer needed his eyes,
I've seen it all.

And like the blind man,
My inner visions prevail,
And from visions come experience,
From experience comes wisdom
And from wisdom comes help.

Let my visions be your visions
Let my experience be your experience
Let my wisdom be your wisdom
And let my help guide you
Through your obstacles
Whatever they may be.

I'll close my eyes
And be blind.

John R. Palmer

The Captive Heart
©1988

This is my voice.
But the things it says
Are often confused.

This is my heart.
And since the heart
Has no voice but actions,
It endeavours such.

But since the brain controls actions
Just as it controls the voice,
The soliloquies of the heart
Are often waylaid
By the actions of the mind.

John's note: perhaps I studied a little too much Shakespeare in high school. As a teen I believed that the soliloquies in plays such as Hamlet were often the most beautiful part of the play, mostly because they were being said by one actor: alone on the stage. To me, this was powerful because I always believed that I was also simply one person, alone on the world stage. However, as "beautiful" as I tried to be in my own actions, I would still mess it up.

Lost
©1987

Somewhere I lost it.
Lost to those baser instincts.

Where's my sense of organisation?
    Lost to laziness.
Where's my sense of love?
    Lost to lust.
Where's my sense of need?
    Lost to desire.
Where's my sense of accomplishment?
    Lost to mediocrity.
Where's my sense of one-ness?
    Lost to external pressure.

Upon succumbing to the need for others
I lost my life.

The Candle
©1989

Here
Alone
I can sit in my corner
And think about
Nothing.

No laughter to cheer
My soul.
No darkness to put fear
Into my mind.

Devoid of stimuli
I can slow the mind down.

The candle burns
Stare deep into its light
It does not burn the eyes

It is the light of warmth,
Of knowledge,
Of ages past.

Inside the light are
Many secrets
To be shared with me.

The secrets of the world
Are mine
To blow out.

Funny how it goes
Up in smoke.

Blue
©1987

These eyes:
Bright blue
"Pretty" blue.
Blue.
They seem to lack expression,
But oh, they are so full!
Listen to my eyes,
They tell a tale of woe.

They speak of caring:
For you, my friends,
My colleagues,
The people I deal with each day.
And you, though I may not know you,
I care about your well-being.

They tell of pain and grief:
Of tragedies, lost loves,
Battered children …
Oh God, why?

Look through these eyes!
And let me express my feelings
To you.

Diary of a Lunatic–Part 1
©1986

The synapses spread
Further apart. What?
What
Was I thinking about?
Flood: life,
Love, friends
Help!?
Drain: where was I?
Confusion! Hold me,
Or what do
I want?
Stay. Come. Go.
Hither. Thither. Who?
Pressure: yes!
No! I don't
Know?

Diary of a Lunatic–Part 2
©1986

Recede! The worms retreat.
Breaking their contact
Forever.
Numb.
Oppressed.
Suggestion becomes fact.

Think about it
(if you still can)

Diary of a Lunatic–Part 3
©1987

Pressure!
Pressure too great,
The mind explodes;
The mind erodes.

Laugh. Ha!
I never seem to smile anymore.
Anymore.

Fill my head,
Think, think, think:
Drink.

The mind departs
Leaving will unchecked.

John's note: sometimes you think you might be crazy, and I spent much of my high school life thinking that I was. This was because I found myself torn between trying to be accepted by people, and trying to be myself. Honestly, I do not think that anything caused more strife growing up than this simple dichotomy. Some of the people in my school were idiots, but everybody liked them. Every day I asked myself "how can I be liked, but not be an idiot like them?" Since I was able to ask myself these questions, I knew I was not actually crazy.

John R. Palmer

A Realization
©1988

I am alone.
Not just alone,
But all alone.

No one to worry
If I made it home okay;
No one to ask
If I had a rough day.

Nobody to care for,
And nobody caring about me.
Nobody to dream about,
And nobody dreaming about me.

I am alone,
With no one to learn to love
But myself.

This could take awhile!

Maybe then,
I'll be good enough for someone else.

Perfect
©1988

The perfect sale:
The perfect presentation of
The perfect amount of
The perfect information about
The perfect product by
The perfect manufacturer with
The perfect uses for
The perfect person in
The perfect world.

With all this necessary perfection, it's hard
To sometimes realise where it ends.

And for you, you deserve
The perfect person.
That's what I tried to be
It's an honourable goal, isn't it?

Except that I mistook
The perfect person
For the perfectionist person,
And I cannot seem to find the line in between.

John's note: I started working in retail at about age eleven. Before I was fourteen, I was responsible enough to run a store for a few hours by myself regularly while the owners were away. It was a perfect metaphor for my life–after all, I was selling myself to people too! The difference was that I was actually *good* at selling products. I became so focused on my early retail career that I was unable to put the store behind me at the end of the day. All I ever talked about was the store and the customers. I worried about the store when I was not there. I found out the hard way that this is not healthy for relationships, because whoever is in your life deserves your attention too.

Appreciated
©1988

Is this what it's all about?
A lack of recognition
For the work I do;
A failure to notice
My commitment,
My input,
My productivity,
The success I've brought!

Has anyone said
"Good job, John,
You're doing okay."
The occasional pat on the back,
Or a small token
That says that you realize
That my actions are needed,
Are noticed,
Are appreciated.
That's all I ask.

John's note: we all like to be acknowledged for what we do, but it is not always going to happen. Even now, I still do not always get acknowledged for the good things that I think I do at home, and at work. I could be waiting a long time if I decide to sit around and mope about it. Instead, I move on–knowing I did my best, and try to do better the next time. After all, maybe what I thought was awesome was only considered to be "just good enough" by someone else, which is probably why the cheers and praise did not come.

Empty Apartment
©1988

Coming home
Down the stairs
Key in the lock

Pause.

Deep breath.

Sigh.

Here I go
Open the door
What a mess.

Drop the coat
Anywhere. Everywhere.
Maybe I should clean up.
Nope.

Check the phone:
No messages.
No calls.
Nobody.

Sigh.

Open the fridge.
Cold pizza, beer.

Jeez,
What am I doing?

John's note: I live in an area where the legal drinking age is nineteen. I was living on my own by the age of eighteen, and having beer in the fridge at age nineteen was not inappropriate when used safely. How lonely (and broke) was I that all I had was beer and pizza in my fridge? Very lonely and very broke.

Tick Tock
©1988

We all live life once,
If we're lucky.

Does this sound like a depressed man?
What does a depressed man sound like?

Like a time bomb?
Tick tock,
Tick tock
Ready to blow up?

I can laugh!
Sure I can laugh!
I tell the jokes,
I smile all the time:
But who's laughing at me?

I wish someone would smile at me
And mean it.
Tick tock.

What am I doing to myself?
Tick tock.

Where am I going?
Tick tock.

Am I really getting by?
Tick tock,
Tick tock.

Maturity
©1989

There's a time
In one's life
When the errors of the past
Become the building-blocks
Of tomorrow

And the true sign
Of maturity
Is the ability
To use each block
To make your life
Full and complete

Taking all of
Your mistakes
To build your path
To walk and live
A perfect life
With the one you love.

Relationships and Love

Is there any topic more important yet more confusing in the life of an adolescent than relationships? From how we get along with our parents, to our dealings with classmates, and the continual search for friends, relationships are key. Throughout the teen years we also move from the confusion of first love, first kisses, the taboos of sex, to the beginnings of our truly adult relationships. None of this is easy on any of us, and each type of relationship seems to be in direct opposition to all of the others.

Where is She?
©1989

Does she dream
That I'm with her?
Does she kiss her pillow
Wishing it was me?
Does she think about me
And smile?

Does it make her
Giggle for just a moment?
Is there a far off
Look in her eyes?
Does she pretend
That I'm with her?

Does she hug her knees
As if they were me?
Does she miss
Me now?
Does she fall asleep
With a smile on her face?

If she does,
Who is she?
     Where is she?
How do I find her?

Words
©1989

There are words:
Words I'd like to say
And things I'd like to do.

Somebody, take my heart.
Somebody, take my soul.
Someone has to let me say
And do these things
That I can only do for you.
For you.

For you, that certain someone,
For you my heart and soul,
For you, I lose my reserve.

Here I am
Heart open wide
My mind looking for an awakening
My life looking for an answer.

Are you there?
Or does my heart ask too much?
Does my soul condemn me
To empty relations?
Does my mind search for one
Who doesn't exist?

Are you an unattainable entity
Is the embodiment of my life
Only an empty space;
A non-existent being?

John R. Palmer

Yes, I will search
And someday say those words
And someday do those things
And someday I will give you all.
Because you are there,
I can feel it.

I Beg of You
©1984

There is naught I can do.
I love her, but she loves you.
While she loves you, and you her,
I haven't a chance.

I know she cares for you,
And you make her happy.
That's what counts.
That's what hurts.

So won't you let me care for her
And make her happy?
I could do it, you know.
I'm not some infatuated child!

You cannot see her, while I can.

So why not let someone else
Love her,
Care for her,
Be with her.

Can't you see that someone
Loves her maybe more than you do?

John R. Palmer

I Beg of Her
©1984

I am a fool!
I love her, but I know she loves him.
So I have promised her
That I will do nothing to stop that love.

But it seems that I can't do anything
Without breaking that promise.

Whenever I talk to her,
Whenever I'm with her,
I always do something
That revokes my promise.

Perhaps she will see me
With all my love
And see how this makes me so
Empty,
Confused,
Loving.

And maybe she'll see that I am what she needs.

Not him.

John's note: these last two poems are obviously related. What do you do when the "perfect" person is right in front of you, but they are already involved with someone else? What do you do when you think that you can treat them better than that other person can? Can you talk to their boyfriend/girlfriend, and tell them to go away? No. Can you try to steal the person away? Not without serious repercussions. What you can do is to simply be a friend, be yourself–at some point in the future, he or she might choose you, but they will only do that if you have proven to be calm, rational, and a good friend. People do not change their mind–they make a new decision based on new information. Be someone worth choosing. If they do not eventually choose you, then it is *their* loss.

Preservation
©1984

So.
Now you've broken up.
What do I do now?

I don't see myself as
good enough to replace him.

Yet, I want to.
But I can't.
No. I can't.

I care about you.
I share things with you.
I help you,
I laugh with you …

Ah, the four main parts of friendship.

Maybe that's the one thing
That I want to preserve.

John R. Palmer

The Kiss
©1984

Have I harmed her,
Or have I harmed myself?

A small kiss: was it all that much to ask?

A hug? No, that was her idea.
Holding hands? That was nothing really.

So why do I feel so bad
After such a small, small kiss?

Why?
©1988

Why am I so nervous?
I know I really like you,
And it seems that you feel the same.

I want to take you,
To hold you,
And have you.
You are what I want.

But my feelings just won't
Express themselves as a spoken word.

I want to kiss you
And express my love.
I want to hug you
And feel you close.

But why can't I do these things
And set my heart at ease?

John R. Palmer

I'll Be Your Everything
©1988

I want to be
Everything that you
Want me to be.

I'll be your friend
Through thick and thin
We'll stay together.

I'll be your brother
And pester you, but you'll know
It's because I care.

I'll be your sister
You can tell me your secrets
And you'll know that they'll stay with me.

I'll be your mother
To cook and clean and care
And be there when you want to talk.

I'll be your father
To be firm and strong
But fair and loving, just the same.

I'll be your lover
Gentle and kind
Giving you all you want.

Roll these together
And you'll get me
Everything that you want me to be.

Worthy
©1988

You see the world
Through your pretty blue eyes
You know you're not blind
To the cheat and the lies.

You've come back to reality,
Because it's the best way, but
You're no further ahead
Than before you went away.

You hid behind masks
And you hid behind dreams
You hid your true self
And right now it seems

That whatever you do
And whatever you say
Things never do seem
To quite go your way.

But the times has come now
To forge your way ahead,
Try to get what you want
And get what you said.

You've found what you want
And you've found what you need.
You know you're not strong
But you know you believe

There are things worth caring for
And things worth a fight,
You've made some mistakes
But you know that's alright.

John R. Palmer

Because today is today
And tomorrow's tomorrow,
This isn't the time
For self-pity or sorrow.

It's time for confidence
And it's time for strength
Because you're in for a job
That could be of some length.

Caring doesn't come quick
And it doesn't come easy
You must show that girl
That you truly are worthy.

And if she feels you are
And she starts to care
Then you know that your journey
Was well worth the fare.

Should I, Do I?
©1988

Are there things that I can say
Are there things that I can do
Is there any little thing
That will help me get to you?

'Cause I don't know how to act
And I don't know what to say
I just want to do the right things
So that you don't run away.

      Should I hold you?
      Should I kiss you?
      Should I never let you go?

      Do I bug you?
      Do you need me?
      Should I even be around?

I just want to be me
And I want you to be you
And I hope that we're compatible
'Cause I want to be with you.

But let me know if you've had enough
And tell me if you want more
'Cause I'm ready to treat you like
You've never been treated before.

So here I stand one of a kind,
Waiting to hear what's on your mind.

John R. Palmer

What is Perfect?
©1986

We all spend so much time
Following the "perfect one"
Who ends up being not
So perfect in the long run.

Then when we're down and lonely
Just looking for a friend,
It sure is nice to look around
And find love in the end.

I'm not saying I could be yours
I know I'm not enough,
But I sure wish you could be mine
And give you all my love.

And now I know my feelings.
I now know that I care.
I'm looking forward to my future,
And I want you to be there.

I know that you're not "perfect",
I don't want you to be,
But for me, you are just what I want
And I want you just for me.

I admit I'm rather greedy
Talking about forever,
But maybe just for a short while
We can be together?

In a Turbulent Sea
©1986

Lost in a wave of emotion,
Escaped from the meaningless self.
Living beyond the barriers of conscience.

Lost in an ocean of faces,
Smiles detached from their thoughts.
Putting on their masks of innocence.

Lost in a flood of strange feelings,
Can you care about someone so much?
Casting adrift on a dream.

Lost in a current of people,
Caring about one, then another.
Breaking the rules of the game.

Lost in a whirlpool of thoughts,
Someone you really do love.
Will you get her, or drown?

John R. Palmer

I Want to Help
©1985

I can see into the night
As clear as if it's day.
I can tell wrong from right
And mould my life that way.

I can see into your head,
And thoughts that there do wander.
In the darkness, in your bed,
I know the things you ponder.

I can see you where you hide,
You want to leave this world.
Your darting eyes are open wide
You're a frightened little girl.

I can see it in your soul
That endless quest for love.
Someone to make your life seem whole:
A blessing from above.

I can see it in your eyes,
You've finally found your key.
Someone has answered all your cries
The faithful one—it's Me!

I can see another place
Where peace and love to reign.
A smile will come to your face,
And rest unto your brain.

And the lion shall lay
Its head down with the lamb.

Trapped
©1985

You are the huntress
With love as your prey
You are on my trail
Ev'ry single day.

Out in the woods
And down through the town
I know it's me
That you're hunting down

    But I won't be trapped
    By no one again.
    Love's been too hard
    I can't stand it again.
    You can try all you want
    But you won't get me
    If you lay your trap
    I'll just break free.

Oh you can shoot
But you can't hurt me
I've been hurt so much
I've gained immunity

You can throw your net
I'll just get out
You can call on the phone
But I'll just shout

That I won't be trapped
By no one again.
Love's been too hard
I can't stand it again.
You can try all you want
But you won't get me
If you lay your trap
I'll just break free.

When you come close, I run away
You keep coming back, every day
You're gaining on me, I'm losing ground
I am the rabbit, run down by the hound.

So now I'm trapped
Trapped again
And I know this time
That love won't end.
I'll stay with you
If you stay with me
We'll have our love
For eternity …

John's note: although this was not my first attempt at a song-lyric style of writing, it is probably one of the best examples of my early attempts. Even now when I write songs, I often brainstorm around a theme—in this case, hunting. After writing down about thirty to fifty words or concepts related to that theme, you generally have most of the words you will want to use. I have never written any music for this early song, which is probably a good thing.

I Must Know
©1987

Is "love" too strong to say?
When I whisper into your ear
"I love you my dear"
Does it make you happy?
I long to know.

If I could find other words
I would say them unto you.
But I cannot find different words
That tell the tale so true.

What thoughts are in your mind?
When I tell you that I care, and that
I need you very much?
What do you tell yourself?
I need to know.

We get along so well,
We're puzzle pieces that fit.
You haven't left me yet
So you must care a bit.

"What is it that you want from me?"
Is what you always ask of me;
I want to be with you.
And so I ask the same.
I want to know.

      Is a kiss too much to ask?
      Am I going far too fast?

We have so much to learn
And I want to have the time.
Tell me what to do,
And spend some time with me.

John R. Palmer

Affected
©1988

I've never had another's life
Influence me so much
My actions are all completely based
On everything you do.

Are you leaving? Are you staying?
My heart wants to know.
Whether I should feel this way
Or should I let you go.

Every time I see your face
I get so flustered
Seeing the things you do, your attitude
I want you more and more.

I long to see you every day
I long to have you near
I long to kiss you, hold you, love you
And care for you alone

I really get confused sometimes
I often get quite scared
That I've done something to scare you off
I try to do what's right.

Is it Just a Dream
©1989

Living here alone
I was sad and uncaring
Didn't need to know
What day it was.
Didn't really care
If the sky was falling
Wasn't really sure
About anything at all

>The days went by and time went past
>Losing my mind I was falling fast
>Now I'm caught up in a dream
>Or is it reality?
>
>Is it just a dream
>A dream I'm having
>Is it just a dream
>A dream I'm living
>Oh can it be a dream
>A dream I'm sharing
>With you.

When we first met
I saw in you
Some kind of pain
But you couldn't let it through
Years of hurt
And years of pain
Memories of being used
Were going through your brain

John R. Palmer

Then you entered my heart
And you entered my mind
'Cause I know that we
Are two of a kind
Now you entered my life
And now we're a team
It feels so good
But sometimes it seems

    That it's just a dream
    A dream I'm having
    That it's just a dream
    A dream I'm living
    Yes it's just a dream
    A dream I'm sharing
    With you.

Mutual Life
©1986

It was yesterday I saw you
And I already miss you.
I need your smiling face.

Last night I dreamed about you
A pleasant dream it was.
I need you tonight.

All morning I've thought of you
And things that we could do.
I need to see you soon.

And so today I called you
To talk for just awhile.
I need to hear your voice.

Again tonight I'll meet you
And have you by my side.
Do you need me at all?

John R. Palmer

A Kiss By Any Other Name ...
©1984

If any girl were to ask me:
> "How many kisses must I give
> to satisfy you?"

I would in reply say:
> "How many grains of sand are there
> on all the beaches of the world?"

If you, my love, were to ask me:
> "How many kisses must I give
> to satisfy you?"

I would in reply say:
> "One."

Not that one kiss is all I want!
If the Gods wished it, I would take one million kisses from you.

All I mean is that at the moment of that one kiss
I would know that you love me.

And I would be satisfied.

Posé pour l'amour
©1985

Comment savez-vous
Si l'amour est vrai?
Y'a t-il un trou
Quand vous-êtes separés?

Quand vous dormez
Révez-vous de lui?
Quand elle t'appelle
Fait ton coeur la bruit?

Pouvez-vous penser
Sans son image?
Ou est votre tête
Au milieu des nuages?

(Il y'a une chose
Que prie à toi
Ne parte pas
Seulement aide-moi)

John R. Palmer

Asked in the Name of Love
Translation ©2006

How do you know
If love is real?
Do you feel a hole
When you're apart?

When you sleep at night
Do you dream of her?
When she calls
Does your heart skip a beat?

Can you even think
Without seeing her face
Or does your head
Remain in the clouds?

There is one thing
That I pray of you
Please never leave
But help me.

Rien peut défendre
©1985

Le mals choix
Sur les rues troits
Ne défendent contre mon amour pour vous.

Les grands mers
Ou les barrières
Ne défendent contre mon amour pour vous.

Les problems quand
Il y'a du vent
Ne défendent contre mon amour pour vous.

Un violent siège
De la niege
Ne défendent contre mon amour pour vous....

Nothing Can Prevent It
Translation ©2006

Poorly made choices
On narrow paths
Won't prevent my love for you

Wide-ranging seas
Or barriers
Won't prevent my love for you

The problems when
The winds blow strong
Won't prevent my love for you

A vicious siege
Of blowing snow
Won't prevent my love for you

John R. Palmer

Metamorphosis of a Soul
©1985

I can feel it!
The warmth of a hold
As feelings flow without words.

I can hear it!
The music of love overwhelms us
As the passionate silence continues.

I can smell it!
The dew on the grass enhances us
As our souls flow into one.

I can see it!
Your smiling face tells me it's true
As we envelop ourselves in magic.

I can taste it!
The air and the water carry the feeling
As the world joins in.

La vie complète (The Complete Life)
©1989

There are many things
We've been through together
And many more to come
Because you know I love you
And you know I'll stay with you
If you'll stay with me
La vie complète.

In my life
There are many things
That influence me strongly
But there's nothing else
That has touched me more
Than the time we've spent

>Walking, talking, laughing
>Crying, lying together
>With nothing around but each other.

Don't ever take that away
Because you know I love you
And you know I'll stay with you
If you stay with me
La vie complète.

Spaces
©1988

I'm sorry.
I never asked if I could take up
This space in your life.

I'm sorry, I should have.

I guess that I was hoping
That I was filling up an empty space there;
A vacant hole in your heart,
And in your mind.

I guess that I was hoping that I was needed.
(We're allowed our hopes.)

It's a lot to ask.
I know that I'm not easy to get along with,
But I care, oh God I care.
But if that's not what you want,
I'm sorry. I can't help it.

If you decide
That you have no room
In your heart, in your mind,
And in your life for me
Then I'll have to accept that.

But if you find
That I belong in your heart,
And that there's room in your mind,
And that I fit into your life,
Then I'll accept that too.

Then I can care for you
And do all the things that will make you proud to say:
"We're together"

Let Yourself Go
©1987

If you tell me to go,
      I'll go.
I want to stay!
To hold you,
To have you,
To love you.

      Let me live!
      Let me love!
      Let me do what
      I have to do.

When the world has got you low
      Don't go.
Stay here and play!
To hold life,
To have life,
To love life.

      Let me live!
      Let me love!
      Let me do what
      I have to do.

When love tells you not to say no,
      We'll go.
Live life each day!
To hold love,
To have love,
To love love!

I will follow.

John R. Palmer

Flesh
©1987

Flesh upon flesh
And more flesh upon more flesh.
The body tingles with excitement,
Expectation.
More, more! Give me more!
More skin to touch.
My arms stretch to
Envelop your body.
God, this is …
Amazing.

The Fall of the Weak
©1987

Sleep my love, sleep.
Rest your head on my lap,
close your eyes,
And wander where only
dreams can penetrate.

I am your protector.
Through this long night,
I shall not blink an eye,
Else the darkness creep into your soul.

You look so peaceful,
Curled up, free of the
problems of the day.
May your dreams take you
where you want to be.

You stir: have I erred?
Have I caused you to
Leave your tranquil state?
No; so I maintain my silent vigil.

The night passes slowly.
All the while you slumber,
sleep attacks my body.
"I must sleep," but I mustn't:
I must keep you safe.

I cannot fail! I have
Accepted this role of protector.
I cannot let my own fatigue
Keep me from my labour of love.

John R. Palmer

The night drains upon
My weary body. Swirling around
the distant realms
Of conscious/unconsciousness.
Though I must remain awake.

My love, I fail.
And if I fail you in this,
Then I have failed you in love.
I succumb to sleep.

The Smile on Your Face
©1988

Not long ago
You smiled when I came to your door.

Even though we'd only been apart
For a few minutes
Or even an hour.

You had that look that said
"I missed you,
I'm glad you're back."

When I think about it
It was that smile
That kept me coming back.

That smile said that you cared
And maybe even
That you loved me.

It was a quiet smile
But to me it said everything
That I needed to hear.

It meant that you were happy to see me
And happy to be near me
And happy that I'd be back again.

At the end of a long day
It told me that
Everything would be okay.

When I needed a little help
To make it through a crisis
I could count on that smile
To support and comfort me

John R. Palmer

Now I'm back again,
I care, I missed you,
I'm happy to see you,
I've had a bad day,
And I can see another crisis coming....

But where's that smile?

Hanging on the Line
©1988

I waited for your call today.

I thought that maybe
We could go to a show
Or maybe have a picnic.

Or perhaps we could go for a drive
Or take a walk in the park.

I was hoping that we
Could talk and laugh
Then talk and laugh some more.

Or maybe sit against a tree
And think quiet thoughts.

Later we could watch the stars
And be alone in the darkness.

I was looking forward
To spending time with you

Which is what I like to do
However we spend it,
Whatever we do.

I waited for a call that never came.

John R. Palmer

Conflicting Voices
©1985

I say hello,
> you say hi.

I say let's go out,
> you say great.

I say love,
> you say lust.

I say friends
> you say sure.

I say hello,
> you say goodbye.

The Lovers Creed
©1986

You want to touch the sky
You want my help to do it.
I really don't know why
But you always make me do it.

    You grow
    With much success you grow
    You say I'm you man
    Then with my hand
    You build your world.

You want to take over the world
You want me to lead your army
With our flags unfurled.
Then you'll take all the glory.

    You grow
    With much success you grow
    You say I'm you man
    Then with my hand
    You rule your world.

You want to break Death's doors
You want to live forever
Sending me to settle your scores
So your death will come never.

    You grow
    With much success you grow
    You say I'm you man
    Then with my hand
    You ask the world.

John R. Palmer

Your time has come to die
You can't be here any more.
You say "let's ride the sky!"
But alone, you pass those doors.

    You grew
    With much success you grew
    You said I was your man
    Then with my hand
    You destroyed yourself.

Next Steps
©1988

You're going now.
The way is clear,
Success lies ahead.

You've found what you want.

We've only met
Things just seemed to
Be going so well.

I've found what I like!

I know I'm not
The perfect guy
I'm not the best.

I do all that I can.

In you I see
A special girl
For whom I've searched.

You're worth working for.

So what do I do now?

John R. Palmer

Bonne Chance (Good Luck)
©1988

Good luck, my love
Bonne chance.
The chance of a lifetime.

For away, the forests stretch
Holding prospects of success.
They call, you must follow.
Follow your dreams!

Be strong, you shall conquer.
Stand tall, you shall top the others.

My thoughts are with you
Wishing you success.

Good luck, my love
Bonne chance.

John's note: sometimes you just have to let them go, no matter how hard that seems.

For Those
©1988

For those who cry
At the time their love is leaving:
I know how you feel.

I short time ago I met a girl:
A special girl,
A girl that's one of a kind.

I fell for her, oh, God, I fell.
But that's okay,
We're allowed to someday.

She's the kind of girl you could love
Like your mother or sister
With respect and grace:
The way a girl like that should be treated.

Somewhere inside of her I'm sure
There's a part of her
That wants to be held and loved.
There is in all of us.

>   I wonder if there's part of her
>   Way down deep inside
>   That may wish she wasn't going?

I got so jealous when she'd talk of friends
Willing to fight if they tried to take her away.
But you can't fight what doesn't exist.

In a way I'd hoped she'd get the job
In another way I didn't.

John R. Palmer

I guess it's what she's looking for
A guess it's what she needs
Maybe someday when she's got her money
She'll find she needs something more.

For those who cry
At the time their love is leaving:
I've joined your ranks.

Missing You
©1987

My body misses
> Your soft caress

My eyes miss
> Seeing you there

My ears miss
> Hearing you say

"I love you."

But one part misses you more
It's way deep inside
You've somehow grabbed it
And kept hold real tight

Because my heart
> Longs for you

My heart
> Beats for you

My heart
> Cries for you

My heart
> Misses you

Most of all.

My arms miss holding you tight.
My hands miss touching your skin.
My lips miss kissing you
The way only you can kiss.

(But my heart misses you
> the way only a heart can)

John R. Palmer

Now I Sleep Alone
©1987

There is only one that I need
To make my life complete.

A tear–
Not a rare sight
When I think of her,
How we'll never be together again.

But I'm not allowed to cry
So I must do it
Alone in my room
Lying on my bed.

Oh! The bed–
A symbol of happiness,
Of sharing,
Of caring,
Of togetherness.

A symbol of love.
A symbol of the many times we had.
Now I'm alone.

The bed is so large,
So empty.

To sleep alone
After having slept with love
Is Death.

CREATIVITY

Sometimes, expression is simply expression. You might be inspired by a book, a snowstorm, or anything. Your personal reaction to that situation leads to your own creativity. Of course, creativity also allows you to write something purely fictional, and sometimes even nonsensical. Go ahead! Express yourself!

Today, the Day
©1988

It was a day of days.

With memories of loves and lost loves;
Friends and lost friends,
Situations that we missed
And chances that we took.

With reminiscence of sunsets and violent storms;
Pleasures, fear, and pain,
Tasks that we failed
And education that we gained.

A day of beginnings and of ends;
Of changes, and of remaining the same,
Of the future, and of the fading past.

But today is the day that is today
Not tomorrow; not yesterday,
And all things come of today.

To a Sunset
©1986

Last night a poem,
        a special verse,
Came flashing through my head,
Ticking my soul,
        my very being,
Like none you've ever read.

I drew my eyes
        towards the sky
To find the very thing,
That Nature's hand
        put in my life
To cause my mind to sing.

And there, yes there,
        a glorious sight,
Oh glory all around;
The swirling colours
        of red and grey
As the sun was setting down.

I sat me down
        upon a bench
And the people passed me by,
But all the time
        my eyes were fixed
Upon the glowing sky.

The clouds they moved
        about the air
As if they were alive,
While the people they
        kept rushing by
Like bees out of a hive.

John R. Palmer

I do not know
        how long I sat
Mesmerised by the sight
But when I stirred
        I became aware
Of a chilly autumn night.

And so I strolled
        through the crowd,
Jostled here and there,
But of the sight
        that was above,
I'm sure they weren't aware.

I took the stairs
        three by three
Still thinking of the poem,
Just thinking how
        to write it down
As soon as I got home.

In through the door
        and to my desk
I sat down in my chair.
I got my pen
        and paper out
But the words: they weren't there!

I searched and searched
        around my head
For those lovely lines,
But the jagged edge
        of nothingness
Was all that I could find.

Like it Or Not

I pined for just
      a moment, then
The answer came quite clear:
That some things are
      too beautiful
For all the world to hear.

But sometimes when
      I'm lonely,
Just staring at the sky,
I hear those lovely
      words again,
And they always make me cry.

John R. Palmer

Sunsets
©1988

The sun's going down
It does nothing to ease my troubled mind.
The beauty of its nightly ritual,
As stunning today as the first time I saw it
… and I've seen a thousand sunsets.

The sun keeps its track through the sky
Oblivious to the actions of the mortals it warms.
What must it think when it views the things we do?

Forever burning, forever giving heat and light
While we trouble below.

Though there is much we have perfected
We will never perfect sunsets.

Elemental
©1983

"Let us come together and create," they said,
"With a portion of each of us three."

"It must breathe of me, else die.
It will be much heavier, though,
So it cannot reach my upper heights."

"It also must drink of me, else wither.
Only it shall be lighter than I,
So that my depths and deepest recesses may not be gained."

"And of my fruits it must eat, else dwindle.
It shall only crawl upon my surface. It must be minuscule,
To prevent domination over my great reaches."

So it was formed: a portion of each
Existing in harmony with the others,
And they marvelled at their co-operation.

"You have been created to please us.
You are a prototype: a perfect union,"
They said to their creation.

"I will drink of the stream;
I will breathe of the air;
I will walk of the land,"
It replied humbly.

For a time, they watched and guarded
Their reverent child.
Seeing that it flourished, they parted
Each to do their respective tasks:

The earth shifted, and replenished its beings.
The water flowed, and replenished its fruits.
The air moved, and replenished its minions.

John R. Palmer

They all failed to notice, until it was almost too late.
Their child, their dearest treasure had grown.

He now moved freely across the land,
Through the air, and under the water.

He set out to conquer his own family
Across the land, sea and air.

He pillaged land, air and sea,
Leaving only pollution behind.

He built weapons to destroy his creators,
Whom he had entirely forgotten about,
Just as they had forgotten him.

The wind noticed that he did not blow as he once had.
"What is happening to me?"

The sea noticed that he did not flow as he used to.
"What has become of me?"

The earth noticed how he had been ravaged extensively.
"What is doing this to me?"

All eyes fell on their monster-child:
The cause of their grief.

"It cannot be!" they cried,
Afraid to admit to having been
Victims of their own.

"We are on the brink of extinction,
We must save ourselves!"

In anger, each withdrew their portion,
Leaving empty shells of all man's toys;
Leaving behind the pollution and destruction.

Like it Or Not

"We shall rejuvenate and rebuild.
Someday, we may try again"

John's note: one of my favourite musicians is Peter Gabriel, and his songs have been a source of influence to many of my songs and poems. This poem is derived from the last few lines of his song *San Jacinto*, but went off in a very different direction than the song, likely because I was also studying Greek mythology at school.

John R. Palmer

Death of a Dreamer-Tyrant
©1983

Only time shall tell what fate shall come
To the armies that march o'er the fields of Babylon.

Through thy weary eyes, they may be strong and great.
But to the trainèd eye, they art but a tribe of staggering fools,
Whose lives have been ruled by an idiot.

A foolish invalid who hath no firm grasp on reality;
A dreamer whose wild fantasies would never show in the worst of fairy tales,
Let alone the best.

A murderer, who through his own stupidity
Has caused the wastage of ten-thousand souls,
While he writhes in his dreams of glory.

Ah, but he shall pay for his stupidity:
Either he will die at the hands of his peoples,
Or he will become more powerful.

Through painful death, he will lose all, and rise to the heavens.

But if he becomes more powerful, his imbecility will destroy his people.
Then, in all his power, he will himself die,
And his soul descend into hell.

John's note: there are a lot of "old style English" words in this piece of prose. As a young teen, I was a big fan of JRR Tolkien's *The Lord of the Rings* series of books. Tolkien was a language specialist first, and a writer second, and tended to write in an older style. As you have noticed, my own creative pieces often have bits of an archaic style because of this inspiration.

The Last Arrow
©1988

The arrow is broken:
There are splinters in my eyes
But they don't blind me.
Alone I hold
An empty quiver.

Many arrows have been spent
Through years of battle
And many used in practice.
Many have been shot foolishly,
And many wide of their mark.
Our aim is not always true,
Though we try our best,
And our hearts are strong.

The battle seemed eternal,
All around, so many fell:
Victims of their own weakness.
With strength I continued
Through their dust and dying rage.
I must go on to make
My final stand.

Behind me many lay.
Behind me the dust has settled
Before me lies my final prey:
My final stand in a weary battle.

John R. Palmer

Alone we stand
In fisted rage
Our weapons aimed
To kill and maim
With strings pulled tight
I cry your name
The final shot
The final game
My final arrow
But yet—no pain?

I release the shaft
From my string
And give to you
The only thing
That means "surrender"
True and real
To show you how
I really feel.

The arrow is broken.
There are splinters in my eyes.
But they don't blind me to love.

John's note: this poem is once again a follow-up to a song, only this time I have mixed some of the concepts of the original song (*Broken Arrow* by Robbie Robertson) with some personal metaphors about life. I have missed my target many times, and there were also times when I probably should not have even tried. In the end, you eventually have to trust someone—and breaking your last arrow and giving it to them is an ultimate example of trust. This poem could have been included with "Relationships and Love", because when you love someone, you are trusting in them. It could also have been included in "Identity", because in many ways it is autobiographical. However, because it closely inspired by someone else's song, I have placed it here as "Creativity", in deference of the original songwriter.

Les étages de la vie
©1985

Où sont les enfants?
En éspace!
Viennent en face
Dans vos places.

Où sont les jeunes?
En autos!
Ils viennent tôt
Vrai ou faux?

Où sont les vielles?
Sur la terre!
Riens à faire
Riens n'est claire.

Où est le monde?
En battre!
On veut être renaitre
Peut-être.

John R. Palmer

The Stages of Life
Translation ©2006

Where are the children?
In space!
Now turn around
Right where you are.

Where are the youth?
Driving cars!
They'll be coming soon
True or false?

Where are the aged?
Well grounded
With nothing to do
Yet nothing is clear.

Where is the world?
In a battle!
One wants to be reborn
Or maybe not.

The Road of Life
©1983

In thy left hand, thou doth hold the past.
As you walk down the paths of life,
Cast it down on the road beside you.

For in thy right hand, thou doth hold the future.
Keep it, use it, it will guide you
Through the rest of your life.

If you should ever traverse this path again,
You may look back upon your past,
Through past hardships and experiences.

Then leave it, and continue into the future.

If the time should come for you to leave this Earth,
You will again travel this path, and pick up your past,
So that you may be whole when you go to the life beyond.

John R. Palmer

In Case of My Death
©1988

Please don't cry over me.
Please don't!

There's nothing you could do.

Who's to say as to
Who's at fault?
We all are, somehow.

I guess I wasn't meant
To go on with this thing called
Life.

But please,
Let yours go on!
Though my candle is extinguished
Let my flame burn in you.

Let my love of life
Spur you on to greater heights
In all that you do.

Don't hide your grief
(If you must grieve);
But let it inspire you
To be all that you want to be.
That's what I've always wanted of you.

Please don't cry over me.
Please grant me this wish.

The Accidental Vision
©1987

It's vividly real
Perhaps my fate
A vision of myself
In an altered state.

Wrapped in bandage
From head to toe
Unconscious,
Perhaps comatose.

In my car
I miss the turn
Vicious impact
Flames that burn.

Grief and death
But not for me
I'm truly sorry
Please don't blame me.

The car! The car!
The steering failed
Leaving me on
A post impaled.

John's note: nightmares can have a very strong effect on you. I used to keep a notepad and pen beside my bed so that I could write down interesting things from dreams. Many times I woke up from horrible nightmares about accidents and wrote poetry (sometimes very sad or disturbing ones) about those very realistic dreams.

John R. Palmer

Drinking and Driving
©1989

Much of our lives are a risk:
Risks that could mean our demise.
Crossing the street
    Lest we be struck by an oncoming car.
Stepping into the tub
    Lest we slip, bang our head, and drown in eight inches of water.
But there are risks
Which we must not take.
There are risks we could lessen.
Drinking and driving:
    Plummeting down a narrow band of asphalt
        In a ton of metal without complete control
            Of your mind and actions leading to
                Injury and death to yourself and others.
    Sure it hasn't happened to you. Yet.
    But next time it just might.
How will you feel when you're told
    That the boy you just hit
        Just didn't make it.
How will his parents feel when they find out
    That all those years of love and hope
        Just ended.
How did he feel when the headlights swerved towards him
    Hearing a thundering crash
        Feeling the shuddering metal
            As he came to a sudden stop?
Or was he even around to feel that?
You never even gave him a chance to say "good bye"
    Even though he didn't want to.
You took that away
You greedy son of a bitch.

John's note: Choosing to drink and drive is a choice that can kill you, and others. Please do not be the next statistic, and choose not to.

Tragedy
©1987

Over in the distance
Where the lights flash red,
There lies a dead man,
Alone on the street.
Why? Why?
Why must he die?

Whom has he injured?
What children harmed?
Why was there no one
To sound an alarm?

On the horizon
The sky turns red.
A single patrol car
Cleans the street.
John Doe.
4th Floor, City Morgue.

Where are his loved ones?
Why haven't they come?
Why is there no one
To tell us his name?

Over in the distance
Where the lights flash red,
In a dingy hospital
A baby is born.
When? Why?
How will he die?

John R. Palmer

Ironic
©1987

Two small boys
Stood on a bridge
Spitting on cars below.

"Watch me" said one
Dancing on the rail,
Only to slip on the
Accumulated spittle.
Plummeting towards the
Traffic below, he thought
"Is this the purpose
Of an overpass, or–".

As the other
Looked upon the crumpled body
He said "I spit on cars
And all they stand for!"

Forgetting that this
Was how it all began.

Lives Given
©1987

Though friends no more,
They once laughed
And cried together.
Ready to give their lives
For each other,
And for us.

Now, resting forever,
They are alone.
No laughter shakes the stones,
And only the tears of others flow.
They gave their lives
For each other,
And for us.

John R. Palmer

Lives Given 2
©1989

The frozen epitaph
Glistens in silent vigil
For those who passed before.

Strong men they were
With icy stares
And warm hearts
Now succumb
To the cold earth
And remain untouched
By the sun's intense heat

Unlike the flowers above
Given as a requiem
To those who once loved
And were loved

With God's help
They will jump forth
To smile upon
The land they fought to save.

John's note: I have always been awed by services held as a tribute to those who have been killed in battle. Growing up, November 11th services were always held in remembrance of wars fought decades ago in countries that seemed so far away. To some people (especially people my age), those wars did not matter. Personally, I was always struck by the ultimate sacrifice that people made. Maybe it is because my father was in the army before I was born, but my sister and I were taught at an early age to respect the war dead. Who knew that years later, those services would include people I have worked with, and that those battles would now be played out on the television news? These last two poems still affect me today in the same way that I was affected when I wrote them, and they are my own tribute to those who sacrificed themselves so that I can sit here and write.

User Guides

Youth Guide

I am going to be completely honest: I am no longer a teen, youth, adolescent, young adult, or whatever term that you or anyone would like to use to describe someone between the ages of thirteen and twenty. I am not a youth now, but believe me, I once was, and I remember it sometimes all too well.

I was a smart (and smart-assed) kid in high school. I was not a high achiever with my marks, and I was certainly not a talented athlete. I was known throughout my school, but friends were few, and I certainly was not going to discuss my problems with them.

I tell you these things because like you, there were times that those things at school were rough. I struggled with who I was, I tried to be different from the crowd, yet be like everyone else at the same time. I also wanted to be "in love", or whatever it was that I thought that meant to me.

Oh, I was friendly with girls, but they had boyfriends, and some of them even used me as a sounding board for their relationship problems. The girls I was interested in either had a "significant other" or wanted nothing to do with me. It did not stop me from trying, and I sometimes tried too hard.

In the midst of trying to be myself, and trying to be with someone else, I had all the other pressures in life: parents, school, acne, part-time jobs—you name it, it probably permeated my waking and sleeping hours.

The good news? I am here all these years later, I am happy with who I am, I have a wife and two young children whom I love, and who love me back.

The bad news? Well, I have been where you are right now, and you might just be in for a few rough years.

There is more good news though: you too can make it through, just like millions have before you.

Every adult on the planet has made it through his or her teenaged years. Cultural differences aside, every single one of them went through the social difficulties associated with moving from childhood to being a responsible adult.

If you look around your classroom, you will see all types of people including the jock, the future homecoming queen, the nerd, the bully, and everything in between. You may have even been labelled with one of these terms.

Like it Or Not

It truly doesn't matter what label you have been given, as every single one of these people in your classroom has to go through their teenaged years, and somehow learn the same skills to be an adult. You might think that the life of a jock is easy, but picture the intense pressure to perform on the sports field, and how quiet it is for them once the cheerleaders have all stopped cheering and gone home. At some point, life is tough on all of us, even them.

What I am trying to say first and foremost is that every single person goes through the pain, confusion, anger and difficulties associated with being a teenager. Most people are able to make it through with only a few scrapes and bruises that will heal and fade with time.

This begs the question however "but how do I make it through?" The first goal of this book is to show you that other have been where you are now, the second goal is to help you to get through it yourself by giving you one of the best coping strategies available: the power of expression.

Reading the Poems

There are books dedicated to "how to read a poem" at the library or bookstore. This is not one of them. These are just a few suggestions that will hopefully help you to see that you are not alone in what you are going through.

Most people who read this book find at least a dozen poems that after reading they can say "hey, that's me", or "oh yeah, that happened to me once." Most will also find a lot more of them where they can say "I know someone who went through that!" This simple idea of identifying with a person or poem is something you already do when you read novels, hear a song, or sometimes watch television.

The first time you read the poems, read each one, do not skip over any because of what the subject matter appears to be. Read the poem simply for enjoyment, follow the flow, and try to understand the message in its basic form.

If you like how it sounds, or the message hits home, read it again, or make a note of it so that you can return to it later.

Even if the poem does not "speak to you" in some way, you may enjoy specific parts, words or ideas in the poem. Just like you might not like the entire episode of a television show, you are welcome to only enjoy parts of a poem.

I challenge you in your reading to find at least a dozen that you can identify with–there are more than ninety in all, so I am sure that you can identify with at least twelve.

Writing Poetry and Prose

Now that you have identified with a few poems, let me say this: you can write better poetry than I can. I do not care if you have never written a poem, or have only written a haiku when your teacher forced you to do it, but I know that you can write a better poem than I can.

I say this if for no other reason but that any poem that you write yourself will mean more to you than anything that me or any other person writes. If you write it yourself, it is yours forever. It may be a snapshot of how you were feeling at the time, and only you know exactly how you were feeling. It is your own personal expression.

So, let us get writing! You can buy a book on writing poems, but rather than tell you what to write or how to write, I would rather just give you some pointers and let you experience writing what you feel.

Format of Poetry

Poetry can be defined as "imaginative writing making use of repetition and rhyme, used to express meaning." Prose can be called the same thing, but that it "resembles speech patterns rather than using poetry structures." There is also such a thing as "free verse", that is essentially "written words recognizable as poetry or prose by coherence or patterns, but without the requirement for rhythm or rhyme." Honestly, who cares about definitions?

What I will say is that it does not matter how you write, it is still valid. You may choose to rhyme, but you may choose not to. Many people like to write like a song with verses and a chorus–it is an easy and recognizable format. Not all of your poems need to follow the same format either. Throughout this book there are poems, prose, songs, free verse–sometimes it just depends on your mood, or the subject matter.

Experiment with your writing styles. Eventually you can challenge yourself to write a song if you have never written one before. Just as the journey of a thousand miles starts with a single step, the journey of writing a poem starts with the first word on the paper.

Other Languages

You may also write your poems in any language. Throughout this book there are a handful of poems that were written in French, which is a language that I learned in school. Although I have provided approximate translations, I do not believe that they are as rich and poetic as the originals. This is not uncom-

Like it Or Not

mon—French, Spanish and many other languages sound very musical, and they allow you to write very different types of verse than writing in English alone.

Subjects to Write About

If you have already read the poems in this book, then you know that you can write about any subject: growing up, love, lust, first kisses, breaking up, anger—the whole range of adolescent (and human) experience.

One of the benefits of poetry writing is that it allows you to take a snapshot of a single moment in our thoughts or experiences, and then write it down in anywhere from ten to one thousand words (or more, if you are so inclined). What you end up with on the page is uniquely yours, although as we have already said, many others have probably experienced something like it. The names, places and specific details have been changed to reflect you, the person who was there.

In other words, if it happened to you, or you wish that it would happen to you, then write about it. If you feel inspired to write a great fictional drama, then write about it. These are *your* poems, so no subject is taboo.

I will however caution against attacking a specific person in a poem. Besides the legal concepts of libel (making nasty comments about someone in writing), scathing personal attacks accomplish very little. Instead, you could write a poem about the *specific actions* that someone does that annoy you, as it can actually help you to look objectively at your likes and dislikes.

Another reason to avoid personal attacks is that occasionally (and often mistakenly) there are outright threats against a person in this type of poem. Spoken and especially written threats towards people are taken very seriously, and should never happen.

Difficult Subjects

There are occasionally subjects or situations that happen that create a whole new level of difficulty for you, and sometimes you are afraid to write about it. Suicide, sexual and physical assault, and any type of abuse are subjects of concern for everyone.

If you or your friends are a victim of assault, or abuse of any type by family, friends, boyfriends or girlfriends, or are contemplating suicide, then someone official *needs* to know right away.

Victims of abuse or assault are often threatened to "keep it secret". You may write poetry that hints at this type of abuse, or you may even write it to yourself in plain, clear language.

Similarly, if you feel overwhelmed or depressed, and have thought about suicide, you may write about the experiences that brought you there. Some people might even write plans for suicide in their poetry.

Let me say that writing about death or a fear of death is not the same as contemplating suicide. You will have read at least a few poems in this book that focus on death, but I never considered suicide, no matter how bad I might have felt.

However, if you are thinking that suicide is an option for you, or if you have been a victim of abuse, it is *vital* to talk to someone that you trust–a parent, aunt, church minister, teacher, police officer or doctor.

If you find the subject difficult to talk about, then show them your poem first. Let them know the situation is serious, and ask for help. By showing them your poems, you can then expand on your hints, or explain your code, and get the help that you both need and deserve.

Showing Your Poems to Others

Now that we have opened the subject of sharing your poems with people, I will emphasize this: your poetry is *your* poetry. Just like a diary or a journal, what you write about is up to you, and only you can choose to share it.

You may send a copy of a poem to your boyfriend or girlfriend, but only if you choose to. You can show your parents a single poem that you are extremely proud of, but not show them anything else–it is your call.

Someday, you may bare your soul, and publish a book of your poems for the entire world to see, but nobody can force you to.

After all, they are *your* poems, *your* thoughts, *your* feelings and *your* experiences. The minute that you put pen to paper, only you can decide to share it with others.

As a teenager, you will experience some tough times. It is not always easy to find someone to talk to, but a pen and some paper are always easy to find. This book will always be here so that you can know you are not alone in your difficulties, and also to help you express your concerns.

You can and will make it through.

Like it Or Not

Parents Guide

Adolescence is Inevitable

If you are the parent of a teen, you are reading this section for one of two reasons. First, you are preparing to give this book to your child so that they may enjoy it, gain some knowledge, and possibly attain some solace through those rough years of your teenager. The second possible reason is that your teenager has bought this book, and is showing it to you so that you may better understand them.

How well do you remember *your* teen years? Most of us have probably tried to forget some if not all of those formative years. Do you remember your first crush? How about that classmate you adored, but who never once looked in your direction? Remember being bullied, teased, or shut out of the "in crowd"? If you were skilled enough to be the high school jock, how empty did life feel with the adoring fans were gone, and the season was over?

Every single one of us went through the trials, tribulations, fumbling and confusion of being a teen. Those few bits that we do remember, we either inwardly or outwardly hope that we could prevent our own kids from facing them.

Guess what? It cannot be stopped. As much as we might like to try and prevent it, our teens have to face being teens, it is an inescapable part of growing up. While we cannot shelter then from the good and bad experiences, the first thing that we *can* do is to prepare them for the possibilities, and be there for them when things happen. Part of the process is letting your kids know that they are not alone.

The teen years are part of that progression between childhood and adulthood, and your teen will be questioning, testing, and sometimes out-and-out rebelling against you. The odds are pretty good that you did it too, so remember that.

Unfortunately (or sometimes fortunately) teenaged kids will rarely share their feelings with their parents. It may be a lack of trust in you, a high level of embarrassment, a belief that you are "not on the same wavelength", or even that some of their concerns revolve around their changing relationship with you. They just are not going to talk.

Therefore the second way to help your child through the emotional rigours of adolescence is to provide them with an outlet for their angst. In some cases this is as easy as giving them someone to talk to, but since they will not talk to you, and may not feel comfortable talking to classmates, many youth automatically turn to diaries or journals. The expansion of simple journals into the creativity of poetry and prose is an easy step that pays benefits for the writer. There is a certain sense of pride and accomplishment that comes with finishing even the simplest of poems.

This book contains poetry and prose written by someone who was experiencing these things first hand. Most teens can personally relate to at least a quarter of these poems, and have second-hand experience with at least a dozen more.

Before Giving this Book

Before you give this book to your kid, I recommend that you read it first. By doing this, you might just remember how challenging your teen years were. As you read it, find two poems: one that speaks to you in some way, and a second that might apply to your child. The first that you choose might be a reminder of your own youth, or a specific concern that you may have for your son or daughter. The second requires you to know your child at least a bit, and you are trying to find a poem that might apply to a situation that your son or daughter is currently facing, or has previously faced.

Now, as you give them this book, have a brief discussion with them. Phrases like "believe it or not, when I was fifteen I felt exactly like the poem on page X ..." not only shows that you are interested, but can open the door to further discussion. You might then be able to say "remember that issue that you had with Tom? I feel that the poem on page Y is how I might have felt in that situation; what do you think?" What a great way to show that you have paid attention to their life, and that you are truly concerned. You have given them the opening to read the specific poem and either agree with you, or tell you that you were way off base. Either way, you have started the discussion into the private life of your son or daughter–just do not force them to reply if they choose not to.

Privacy

When you do finally hand over this book, it is not a bad idea to keep the lines of communication open by saying "look, if you ever write something that you really want me to read, please show it to me. If you want to talk about it, we can, but if not, I promise not to push it."

After that, hand it over and expect to never see it again: ever. Just as you would never read your daughter's diary, do not go looking for your child's poems. The temptation will be there, but do not succumb to it, because it's the surest way of breaking trust.

Subjects of Concern

Once in awhile, your child may show you a poem with a subject matter than absolutely floors you. No matter what, do not jump to conclusions!

For example, your son or daughter may write one or more poems about death. This book alone contains more than a half-dozen poems that use death in a physical or metaphysical sense. Have a look at poems such as "The Quest", "In Case of My Death", or even "Lives Given". One speaks of the metaphor of the death of the individual persona as we integrate into society, the second speaks of a fear of death and concern for those left behind, and the third is a November eleventh-inspired attempt to honour those who have died fighting for peace. Nowhere will you find any desire or hint at plans for suicide.

However, if a series of poems see to focus on death, glorify suicide or killing, or contain an actual threat of injury to themselves or others, then your child could possibly be sending a message. At this point, it is vital to be non-judgemental, and speak in non-value-laden phrases about the subject. When it comes to suicide, any threat *could* be serious, and your child could be asking for help. I recommend that everyone be exposed to the Applied Suicide Intervention Skills Training (ASIST)[1], or a similar workshop on recognizing and preventing suicide. In many cases, you will need to seek professional assistance.

Your son or daughter may also write about situations of abuse. This could range from schoolyard bullying (which may require a discussion with teachers) or very frank descriptions of other forms of abuse. If there is even a slightest hint of abuse, or a hint of something that they cannot tell anyone due to the potential for future suffering, it is vital to act. Many abusers, especially those within the family, will make direct or indirect threats for the child to not tell anyone, "or else". If your child shows you a cryptic poem that seems to hint at an abusive situation, they might be hinting and asking for help.

At times, your child's poetry may also suggest abuse (physical, sexual or mental) at the hands of a boyfriend or girlfriend, and they may again be alerting you to the situation. All suspected cases of abuse need to be handled carefully so as not to increase the risk to your child, but also firmly so that your son or daughter is no longer a victim.

---

[1] For information visit http://www.livingworks.net

Occasionally, a poem that your teen shows you may suggest alcohol or drug use, or inappropriate sexual activity (especially based on their age). These may be fictional "what ifs", or may signify an issue. You will need to have a wider view of your child's activities, and take advantage of an open door to have further rational discussion. In some cases, this may lead to family therapy.

Try to remember yourself as a teen. Think about the environment at home and school that surrounded you. Any action or activity that was available to you is equally if not more readily available to your children.

Above all, encourage your children to express themselves. If they want to talk, then listen. Do not judge them as a person, but discuss activities and risks. If they ask for help, get appropriate help.

Of course, if they need more space to write their poetry, then by all means, buy them something to write in, and throw them in a brand new pen too.

For more youth and parents resources, visit http://www.JohnRPalmer.com

Appendix A—Short Prose and Beginnings

Sometimes a great idea pops into your head, and you put your pen to the paper ... but only a few words come out. Alone, they do not make a full poem, but perhaps some important emotion came out. At other times, maybe your writing was almost more story-like than poetry.

All of these short stories and prose are still very useful pieces of writing. Someday in the future you may go back and finish a half-written poem. You may even hold a one-line comment as your own personal belief.

This section includes a few examples of free verse from a wide variety of subjects that were not quite ready for the big time.

Sometimes
©1988

Sometimes we cannot see the directions we are going.
At other times we're blind to the consequences of our actions.
We run around in circles and hurt those around us.
We walk without purpose while our lives crumble.
We take a lonely path, not knowing where it leads
Until we stand alone in a hostile world.

Hero
©1989

I've seen you in your finest hour: the victor; the champion.
Through the waves of adulation you never besmirched the loser.

I've also seen you when you lose—no blame, no sorrow.
Just the ultimate will to strive for success the next time.

You Can Make It
©1988

Life is not what it seems, although it seems quite sad.
It can be kind of rough, but it's not that bad.
Because life's what you make it, and you can take it:
Everything that comes your way.

John's note: this is probably less of a poem, but more of a "mantra" in poetic form. No matter how bad things seem, and no matter what the world throws in your path, you can make it through.

If Only I Could
©1988

Sometimes I wish that I could live in a town where I could stop at McDonalds for breakfast on the way to work and actually afford it.

Sometimes I wish I could meet a girl. We could do romantic things, tell jokes until we cried, then hold each other until we sleep and do it all again the next day.

Sometimes I wish I could get a job where I could talk and laugh with the people I deal with. They would be happy, get what they needed and feel good about themselves, and so would I.

Sometimes I wish I could do everything I needed to keep myself healthy so that I could live a full life along with those I love.

Sometimes I wish I had the timing to do and say what is required to impress and inform and get the girl I love.

Sometimes I wish I could lead an eccentric life: pick up a wool trench coat, get into a Fiat Spyder and just drive. Wearing John Lennon shades, and charcoal grey pleated pants, I could simply turn up at some long lost friend's house.

John's note: there often comes a point where disillusionment sets in. You have your first real job, but it pays poorly. You might live in a small town, or a far-off neighbourhood, and can barely afford to keep yourself afloat both financially and mentally. You start to think how great it might be to have a movie-ending type of existence. What happens after the movie ends? In real life it means you go back to school or work on Monday and continue on.

Friendship
©1984

How many times do people stay friends after being lovers? Few. Too few. Our friendship is too precious too lose. We could never be lovers, because it would cause the loss of something I really need: a friend.

Like it Or Not

Too Blind
©1986

Too blind to see the love
Too blind to see the hate
Too blind to see deceit
Too blind to admit defeat.

Love Is …
©1987

Love is the ability to share emotion, thus directing the paths of each other's activities thenceforth and forever.

All You Need
©1987

Just hold me, and I'll give you everything: all that you need, all that I can—it's yours if only you will love me.

The Fine Line
©1988

Where does the caring stop and the loving begin? Where do we draw that fine line?
Can we draw it too early? Can we draw it too late? Or do we even need to draw it?

It felt so right to say it, and it seemed like just the time.
That night I said "I love you" I learned that there is no line.

Loneliness
©1989

There's no one around to share things with.
It's not that I set my expectations too high: for if I don't, no one can set them for me.
Am I not looking in the right places? Or is there even anybody to find?

Inevitable
©1988

There are a multitude of ends towards which our lives traverse. Like it or not, one of those ends must occur.

Whether you choose to lead a happy life, or constantly drown yourself in the sorrows of existence is your own choice. If you wish to follow a moral, hypocritical path, continuing to put down those who "live their lives to the fullest", that is your choice, and yours alone.

Whichever way you choose to exist, it does not sweeten the fact that at some point you will cease to exist. At that point it does not matter how you lived, just that you no longer do.

John's note: we often hear that we should "live life to the fullest." That is very true within reason. We may have a right to "life, liberty and the pursuit of happiness", but are we bound by the responsibilities that go with that right–responsibilities to ourselves, our families, our colleagues, and our friends. At the end of our days, will we be known as a great person, or a good worker? Will someone say "he was a good friend" or "she was always willing to help?" We will be forever judged on how we act.

Loser
©1987

Fear not the loser!
He'll do you no harm.
Follow the winner!
Hold him in your arms.

I worked, I tried
I used all of my charms.
Now, fear not the loser
I'll do you no harm.

My Couch
©1988

I sleep on the couch. It's small.
The bed is so big.
So empty.
So lonely.
The couch may be uncomfortable,
But at least I can sleep.

Clairvoyance
©1983

Through thy right eye, I see only joy and happiness.
Through thy left, I see the destruction of the universe and all within.
If you had'st a third eye, I would be able to see the true future,
And all it holds.

Philosophy of Death
©1984

Pain consumes the soul
Until the time comes
That though One seems alive,
One is really dead.
Will-less.
Want-less.
Feeling-less.
Until death becomes a goal
That the body tries to reach.

Appendix B—Writing in Anger

Anger is a completely valid emotion. How we deal with anger is a true sign of who we are as a person. When faced with an angry situation, we can take actions that we will likely wish we had not, or we can deal with the issue internally first and then act calmly later. There is a truly therapeutic feeling to putting pen to paper and expressing our anger and frustration in prose (it is hard to rhyme when you are really angry!).

The following pages of prose were written at a time when I was living six hours from my family, completely broke, and doing poorly in my first year at university. On top of that, I had just broken up with my girlfriend, and had no true friends to turn to in order to talk about it. My life, as a 19 year-old was falling apart (although it did eventually get better).

NOTE: The following three pages contain words and concepts that may be offensive to some readers.

Profound Angry Scribbles
©1987

"The world is screwed: the rodents rule
where ancient scholars once combed
the earth for true signs of economic
wealth, rather than peace"

—

"What matters whither comes the morrow,
for war shall overcome all grief, pleasure,
and passion, leaving me sitting alone
on defective dynamite"

—

"But who cares what happens to me
anyway? All that anyone looks out
for is themselves, not worrying about
who I may care about, 'cos
it's certainly not myself"

—

"What is life without love; love without
someone to love; someone to love without
paying $500 for an hour; $500
without a real job, like screwing the
president, or driving a cab"

—

"Have you ever felt that your life was
the cumulative crap of everyone
who ever lived, except for those
whose lives were important, because
that crap would be forever revered by all?"

—

John R. Palmer

"Why does everything I do get screwed
up either by the minds of the people
who watch, those who carry it out,
or by my own stupid lunatic mind?"

—

"Why is it that when you finally really
love someone, they don't have room for
you in their fecal wastes, Or
any other part of their life, no
matter how meaningless?"

—

"Ever wonder why dogs lick their balls?
It's because their love life lasts one hour,
Tops, so the rest of the time they only
Have themselves to think about: much
like most people I know."

—

"Have you ever felt that you
would kill yourself
immediately—if only the
kettle wasn't boiling?"

—

"Why can't you love someone
without them loving you
back? It's because they'll
arrest you and put you
in jail, where you will
be loved very much"

—

"Have you ever felt like blowing
someone away, even though
they really haven't done
anything wrong, except
insult you behind your back?
Then you stop because you
Love somebody who is
Really important to you?"

About the Author

John R. Palmer is an internationally-known songwriter whose works have been heard in Canada, the United States, the Caribbean, and Scandinavia. His newspaper columns have appeared in newspapers in many major cities.

He is an environmentalist, computer specialist, politician and public speaker, and occasionally leads worship services at a church in Ottawa, Canada.

Like It or Not is his first published work, although an upcoming non-fiction work entitled *Meeting My Friends in Heaven* has already been described as "one of the most important pieces of interfaith understanding".

John lives with his wife Jill, and their fraternal twins Joshua and Juliana in the Ottawa area.

For more information please visit http://www.JohnRPalmer.com

Index of Poems by Year

1977
The Quest, 4
1983
Clairvoyance, 114
Death of a Dreamer-Tyrant, 85
Elemental, 82
The Road of Life, 90
1984
A Kiss By Any Other Name ..., 51
Friendship, 111
I Beg of Her, 33
I Beg of You, 32
Philosophy of Death, 114
Preservation, 34
Reality, 3
The Kiss, 35
1985
Conflicting Voices, 65
I Want to Help, 43
Les étages de la vie, 88
Metamorphosis of a Soul, 55
Nothing Can Prevent It, 54
Posé pour l'amour, 52
Real People, 7
Rien peut défendre, 54
The Eagle Inside, 6
The Stages of Life, 89
Trapped, 44
1986
Are We Individuals?, 10
Asked in the Name of Love, 53
Diary of a Lunatic–Part 1, 19
Diary of a Lunatic–Part 2, 19
In a Turbulent Sea, 42
Mutual Life, 50

Sommes-nous individuels?, 10
The Lovers Creed, 66
To a Sunset, 78
Too Blind, 112
What is Perfect?, 41
1987
All You Need, 112
Blue, 18
Diary of a Lunatic–Part 3, 20
Flesh, 59
I Don't Need You, 8
I Must Know, 46
I Stand, 11
Ironic, 95
Let Yourself Go, 58
Lives Given, 96
Loser, 113
Lost, 16
Love Is …, 112
Missing You, 72
Now I Sleep Alone, 73
Profound Angry Scribbles, 116
The Accidental Vision, 92
The Fall of the Weak, 60
Tragedy, 94
1988
A Realization, 21
Affected, 47
Appreciated, 23
Bonne Chance (Good Luck), 69
Empty Apartment, 24
For Those, 70
Hanging on the Line, 64
I'll Be Your Everything, 37
If Only I Could …, 111
In Case of My Death, 91
Inevitable, 91
Mirrored Life, 12
My Couch, 114

Next Steps, 68
Perfect, 22
Should I, Do I?, 40
Sometimes, 47
Spaces, 57
Sunsets, 77
The Blind Man, 14
The Captive Heart, 15
The Fine Line, 112
The Last Arrow, 86
The Smile on Your Face, 62
Tick Tock, 25
Today, the Day, 77
Why?, 36
Worthy, 38
You Can Make It, 110
1989
Drinking and Driving, 93
Hero, 110
Is it Just a Dream, 48
La vie complète (The Complete Life), 56
Lives Given 2, 97
Loneliness, 112
Maturity, 26
The Candle, 17
Where is She?, 29
Words, 30

978-0-595-50644-6
0-595-50644-5

Jody,

Remember the journey, but live in the destination.